THE SCIENCE OF LIFE

FOOD CHAINS

by Carol S. Surges

Content Consultant
Lee Kats
Professor of Biology
Pepperdine University

CORE
LIBRARY

Printed in the United States of America,
North Mankato, Minnesota
092013
012014
 THIS BOOK CONTAINS AT LEAST 10% RECYCLED MATERIALS.

Editor: Arnold Ringstad
Series Designer: Becky Daum

Library of Congress Cataloging-in-Publication Data
Surges, Carol S., author.
  Food chains / by Carol S. Surges ; content consultant, Lee Kats.
    pages cm. -- (The science of life)
  Audience: 8-12.
  Includes bibliographical references.
  ISBN 978-1-62403-160-1
1. Food chains (Ecology)--Juvenile literature. 2. Predation (Biology)--
Juvenile literature. I. Title. II. Series: Science of life (Minneapolis, Minn.)
  QH541.15.F66S87 2014
  577'.16--dc23
                        2013031885

Photo Credits: Shutterstock Images, cover, 1, 4, 7, 11 (top left), 23, 31, 39,
45; NOAA, 9; Anan Kaewkhammul/Shutterstock Images, 11 (top right);
Eric Isselee/Shutterstock Images, 11 (bottom left), 11 (bottom right); Olha
Afanasieva/Shutterstock Images, 12; Joe Gough/Shutterstock Images, 15;
Red Line Editorial, 18; David Lade/Shutterstock Images, 20; M. Cornelius/
Shutterstock Images, 25; Regien Paassen/Shutterstock Images, 28;
iStockphoto/Thinkstock, 34; Zack Frank/Shutterstock Images, 37; Danny E
Hooks/Shutterstock Images, 42 (top); David Mckee/Shutterstock Images,
42 (bottom); Janelle Lugge/Shutterstock Images, 43

CONTENTS

CHAPTER ONE

USING THE SUN'S ENERGY

Did you know that you are full of the sun's energy? All the energy in the food you eat originally comes from the sun. The energy travels through plants and animals until it gets to you. The path it takes is called the food chain. The energy from the food chain lets you do everything from solving math problems to playing soccer.

Energy from the sun passes through plants into other organisms, including you.

Unlike animals, plants can make their own food. The process plants use to make food is called photosynthesis. They use the sun's energy to combine water with a gas called carbon dioxide. The result is a gas called oxygen and sugars, such as glucose. The sugar is stored in stems, roots, leaves, fruit, seeds, and flowers.

During photosynthesis, the sun's energy is moved from sunlight into the sugar. Animals can't get energy directly from the sun. But they can get energy from sugar. When animals eat plants, energy is released from the food. If you visit a small farm, you will see that cows spend most of their time eating grasses and other plants. The cows are getting energy

Sugar

Sugar is found in many foods. Plants make sugars and animals use those sugars for their energy needs. The sugar in cakes and cookies usually comes from sugarcane or sugar beets. The sugar from these plants is called sucrose. It is processed into the white sugar you can buy at the supermarket.

Cows help move energy from plants to people.

from the plants. They use the energy to make milk and do other things.

When you eat plants or animals, their stored energy moves into your body. You use the energy to move around, grow, and stay healthy. The sun's energy is the fuel that keeps almost all the plants and animals on Earth alive, including you.

Away from the Sun

The sun powers nearly all food chains, but scientists have discovered animals that don't need the sun's energy. These unusual animals live on the ocean floor. In some areas, openings in the ocean floor release very hot water. Animals living here are tubeworms with no mouths. They use extreme heat, minerals in the water, and bacteria to obtain energy. The tubeworms are an important link in a sea-floor food chain. Other deep-sea creatures eat the worms to gain energy.

Studying Food Chains

Scientists study food chains to learn how the sun's energy moves from one living thing to another. The plants and animals in a food chain are connected by the food they eat. These chains exist anywhere that plants and animals live. Forests, oceans, deserts, and other environments all have their own food chains. Studying the interactions between organisms and

Tubeworms at the bottom of the sea are one of the only organisms that do not use the sun's energy to survive.

their environment is called ecology. Scientists who work in this field are called ecologists.

The sun begins nearly every food chain. Plants are the first link in the chain. The second link is an animal that eats those plants. The third link is a different animal that eats the first animal. Food chains on land are often three links long. Food chains in water and in the soil are often longer than that.

Scientists often use arrows to show how energy moves between the links on the chain. For example, imagine a food chain in which a rabbit eats grass and then is eaten by a fox. An arrow from the grass to the rabbit shows the energy moving from plant to animal. Another arrow then points from the rabbit to the fox, showing the energy's continued movement. Food chains are all about the flow of energy. They help explain how animals and plants are connected.

A Simple Food Chain

This is an example of a very simple land food chain. Follow the path of the energy through the food chain. Are there any other paths the energy might take? Could there be another link beyond the fox?

CHAPTER TWO

PRODUCERS AND CONSUMERS

Let's look more closely at the food chain from Chapter One. The first link, grass, is called a producer. A producer is any plant that makes up the first link of a food chain. A producer gets its name because it makes its own food.

The remaining links in a food chain are called consumers. The rabbit and the fox are consumers. Consumers cannot make their own food. They must

Forests are full of producers.

get it from other living things. All animals are consumers.

The first consumer link is called the primary consumer. The primary consumer is always a plant eater. The rabbit is the primary consumer in the example. Rabbits only eat plants, so they are known as herbivores.

The fox in the example is the secondary consumer. Secondary consumers eat the primary consumers on a food chain. The fox eats the rabbit in this food chain. Foxes eat both meat and plants, making them omnivores. Most people are omnivores too. However, some people, called vegans, choose to eat only plants.

Carnivores and Predators

Other animals, called carnivores, eat only meat. Since they don't eat plants, carnivores are always secondary consumers or higher. These animals include frogs, spiders, lions, and sharks. Carnivores are often the biggest and fastest animals in a particular food chain.

Most people are omnivores, eating both plants and meat.

Carnivores can also be predators. These are animals that hunt and eat other animals. The animals they eat are called prey. In the example, the rabbit is the prey and the fox is the predator. A wolf could be added to the chain as a fourth link, called a tertiary consumer. The wolf would be a predator and the fox would be its prey.

Carnivorous Plants

All plants use photosynthesis to make energy. However, some plants can't get all the nutrients they need from the soil. They live in poor soil where important minerals are missing. In order to stay alive these plants eat animals, mostly insects. They use special kinds of leaves to trap their food and digest it. More than 600 different kinds of carnivorous plants get food in this way. A few of them are large enough to trap and eat a whole frog.

Food Chain Models

Scientists use models to understand food chains. They are always looking for better ways to show how food chains work. One model they use is called the pyramid of numbers.

The pyramid of numbers shows the huge numbers of plants needed to support a few herbivores and even fewer carnivores. The pyramid gets narrower at each level. It takes a lot of grass to provide food for a rabbit. There are fewer rabbits because each one uses so much grass. There are even fewer foxes because they eat the scarce rabbits.

Other pyramid models show the biomass of food chains. Biomass is the combined weight of living things. Biomass models work where pyramids of numbers don't. For example, one tree can provide food for many insects. Those insects can then be food for a few birds. With a pyramid of numbers, the first level would be narrow, the second level would be wide, and the third level would be narrow again. But with a pyramid of biomass, the huge tree is the base of the pyramid. The combined weight of thousands of insects is the smaller second level. Finally, the combined weight of a few birds is an even smaller third level.

The pyramid of energy shows how energy moves through food chains. Below the base

Biomass

Insects, such as ants, weigh practically nothing compared to a human being. But the world has many, many more ants than people. Scientists estimate there are more than 1 million ants for every one person on Earth. The total biomass of all the ants in the world is more than the total biomass of human beings.

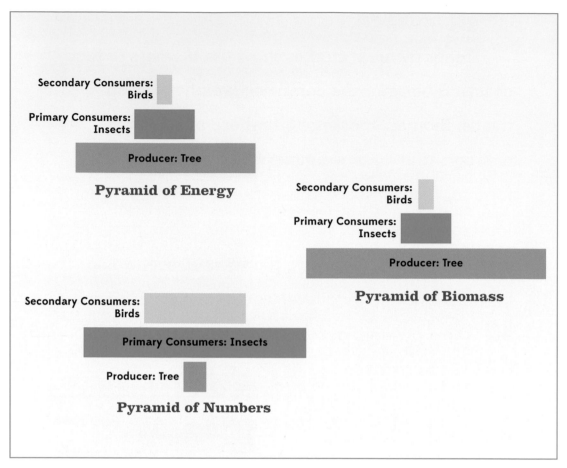

Pyramid Models

Different pyramid models show different relationships between members of food chains. These pyramids all show the relationship between a tree, insects, and birds. Think of another food chain. How would each of the pyramids look when applied to that food chain?

of the pyramid is the energy from the sun. Not all of the sun's energy reaches plants. Some simply goes out into space. This means that the first level of the pyramid, the energy in plants, doesn't contain all of the energy the Sun sent to Earth. Plants use some of this energy to grow and stay alive. Not all of it is stored by plants. So the next level of the pyramid, the energy animals get from plants, is narrower. Energy is lost at every level. The energy pyramid shows that large amounts of energy are needed to keep consumers alive.

CHAPTER THREE

NOTHING IS WASTED

Nothing is wasted in nature. When animals and plants die, other organisms use their bodies. Organisms called decomposers use these dead bodies as food in the last step of a food chain. They break down the dead plants and animals so the nutrients can be returned to the soil and used again by plants.

Decomposers eat away at dead organisms.

Soil Organisms

Much more life exists below the soil than on top of it. In one square foot (0.09 sq m) of garden soil, you might find up to 50 earthworms and dozens of nematodes. And that's just what you can see. Each teaspoon of soil also has thousands of single-celled animals and more than 1 billion bacteria. These are invisible to the human eye unless you use a microscope.

The First Decomposers

Decomposers form a food chain of their own. Some decomposers are called scavengers. They are animals that eat dead animals. Vultures and hyenas are well-known animal scavengers. But crows, blue jays, foxes, and raccoons also act as scavengers. When scavengers have finished eating, other decomposers move in to continue the process.

Worms and insects are the first decomposers to eat dead plants. As the decomposers eat they break the dead material into smaller pieces. This makes it easier for even smaller decomposers to consume the dead material. As decomposition goes

Worms help return nutrients to the soil. These nutrients then help new plants grow.

on, the types of organisms participating become smaller and more numerous.

Smaller Decomposers

Bacteria and fungi finish the decomposing process. Many bacteria and fungi are so small you need a microscope to see them. Decomposing bacteria usually break down dead animals. Fungi are good

Penicillin

Medicines called antibiotics can help people recover from illness. One famous antibiotic, penicillin, is made from a fungus called *Penicillium*. In nature, *Penicillium* acts like a decomposer. It consumes the sugars in dead leaves. It also gives out a chemical that kills bacteria near it. In the human body, penicillin helps to kill harmful bacteria. However, it does not help against viruses responsible for illnesses such as the common cold.

at breaking down dead plants. Plants are harder to decompose than animals. Special fungi are needed to soften the tough plant material. When you see a mushroom on a dead tree, you're looking at part of a fungus. Its tiny hairlike structures are out of sight, breaking down the wood.

People Helping Nature

People sometimes like to help nature along by making compost piles in their backyard. Compost piles are designed to encourage decomposition. They contain things such as soil, dead leaves, and food garbage. If you look closely at a compost pile you

Compost piles should be carefully layered to ensure decomposition happens quickly.

will see many worms, slugs, millipedes, pill bugs, and other organisms hard at work. They are breaking up and eating the plant matter in the pile. What you can't see are the billions of tiny decomposers that are also working in the compost pile. If you put your hand into the middle of a compost pile, you would feel heat. This is the energy being released as the decomposers break down the plant material. Just like the heat your body gives off, that energy is lost from the food chain.

John Muir, a famous naturalist and conservationist, made the following entry in his 1869 journal during the first summer he spent in the Sierra Nevada, a mountain range in California:

> *One is constantly reminded of the infinite lavishness and fertility of Nature—inexhaustible abundance amid what seems enormous waste. And yet when we look into any of her operations that lie within reach of our minds, we learn that no particle of her material is wasted or worn out. It is eternally flowing from use to use, beauty to yet higher beauty; and we soon cease to lament waste and death, and rather rejoice and exult in the imperishable, unspendable wealth of the universe, and faithfully watch and wait the reappearance of everything that melts and fades and dies about us, feeling sure that its next appearance will be better and more beautiful than the last.*

Source: John Muir. *My First Summer in the Sierra. Boston: Houghton Mifflin Harcourt, 2011. Print. 161.*

Consider Your Audience

When Muir wrote in his journal, ecology was not a science. His writing is poetic and full of his feelings about nature. Do you share any of his feelings? How would you use the information and terms you have learned in this book to explain to your friends what Muir was talking about?

CHAPTER FOUR

FROM FOOD CHAINS TO FOOD WEBS

A food chain shows a single path that energy takes as it moves from producers to consumers. However, nature is usually much more complicated than this. Different animals compete for the same food sources. Some animals, such as omnivores, can feed on different kinds of foods. Producers and consumers become parts of many different food chains. The combination of these

Bears eat both plants and meat, putting them in several different food chains.

chains is known as a food web. Food webs give a realistic look at how plants and animals interact in nature.

Different Food Webs

Food webs vary from place to place and climate to climate. A water-based food web has very tiny plants and animals called plankton that are eaten by many different types of fish. In the ocean even some of the largest whales eat these tiny organisms.

A food web near the surface of the ocean will look very different than one deeper in the ocean or even at the bottom. Food webs near the Arctic Circle are very different from those near the equator.

Krill

Krill, tiny animals found in oceans, spend much of their time near the ice of the Arctic and Antarctic. They are there because they can find their food, plankton, in the small pools and openings that form within the frozen sea ice. Krill are eaten by whales. The blue whale, the largest animal ever to live on Earth, can eat up to 8,000 pounds (3,600 kg) of krill each day.

Animals often must find new food sources during winter.

Food webs also change from season to season. In the summer, a food web on a tundra will be very different from one in the same place in the winter. Animals such as the caribou return to the tundra every spring to feast on the fresh food supplies. Many animals hibernate during the winter because they can't get enough food in the cold. Hibernating animals' bodies use less energy.

Insects such as butterflies are in different food chains at each stage of their life cycle. A larva eats different food than an adult butterfly does. Different animals eat larvae than eat adult butterflies.

Insect Shape-Shifters

Dragonflies are predators in the air. They eat moths, wasps, flies, beetles, and bees. Young dragonflies live as nymphs in the water. The nymphs are predators too, hunting and eating small fish and other water animals. These two stages of the same insect belong to very different food chains and food webs.

CHAPTER FIVE

A CONNECTED WORLD

Our complex, connected natural world is changing quickly. More animals and plants are becoming endangered or extinct than ever before. When trees are cut down for farmland or manufacturing, habitats are lost. The climate is changing, causing polar ice to disappear. Scientists are concerned about these changes. One thing scientists have discovered is that every link in a food

Melting polar ice threatens food chains in the Arctic.

chain is important to all the other links. If just one animal in a food chain goes extinct, the chain can fall apart. Other plants and animals that rely on it may go extinct too.

Extinct Giants

At one time huge mammals roamed North America. They included camels, mastodons, giant beavers and sloths, saber-toothed cats, and more. The giant sloth was approximately 20 feet (6 m) long from head to tail. Saber-toothed cats had teeth approximately eight inches (20 cm) long. But about 13,000 years ago, these huge mammals all went extinct. Most scientists think they disappeared because of climate changes and overhunting by humans.

Wolves at Yellowstone National Park

An example of what can happen when a food chain breaks down can be seen in North American wolves. At one time, wolves roamed from the northeastern states through the Midwest and all the way to the West Coast. As early as the 1600s, farmers wanted to get rid of them. The wolves were eating their livestock.

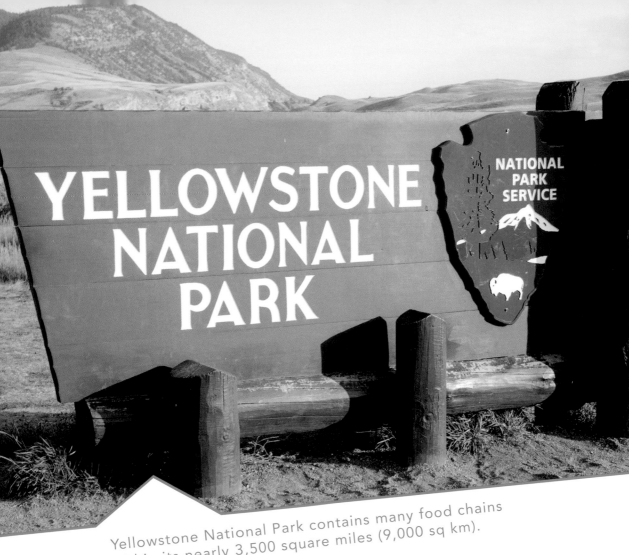

Yellowstone National Park contains many food chains within its nearly 3,500 square miles (9,000 sq km).

The farmers began hunting and poisoning the wolves. By the 1860s, no more wolves were left in the eastern United States. Other parts of the country did the same thing. By 1926 even Yellowstone National Park had very few wolves left.

Before long, the elk that grazed on the plants in Yellowstone were growing in number. There were not enough wolves to keep the elk population down. Plants were being eaten too quickly. New trees did not have time to grow before elk chewed them down. The park's habitat was changing. The government brought hunters in to bring the elk population down, but it wasn't enough. The problems continued. By 1995 scientists realized the wolves had to be brought back into Yellowstone.

Today Yellowstone National Park is getting back into balance. The wolves' numbers are growing, and there aren't as many elk to cause serious damage to the plants that grow there. New trees are filling in the forest again. The park is looking more like it did before the wolves left. This is just one example of what can happen when one link of the food chain is taken out of food webs. There are many more examples all over the world.

Bringing back wolves helped repair the food chains in Yellowstone.

Understanding Problems, Finding Solutions

Removing predators, such as wolves, can be disastrous. But a link removed from any part of a food chain can cause problems. Sometimes problems can also begin at the bottom of a food chain when plants are eliminated from a habitat. When scientists notice

The Mysterious Missing Honeybees

In 2006 beekeepers noticed that thousands of honeybees were dying. As soon as the word got out, scientists worked to discover what was killing them. The problem was not easy, and scientists are still searching for an answer. It appears many things are responsible. Pesticides, diseases, and other insects may all be to blame. Whatever the reason, the lack of honeybees will hurt many food webs. The bees are very important pollinators. They make it possible for many plants to reproduce.

that animal populations are shrinking, they know the ecosystem is running into trouble. They must study the entire food web to understand what is happening and why. The interactions between animals, food webs, and habitats can be very complex.

Finding the answers to these problems is not easy work, but it is important. If we want to keep the plants and animals we have, we must know how to protect them. The more we learn about food chains, the more we realize how connected all of Earth's life is.

In an interview, ecologist Sylvia Earle was asked why the ocean is so important to life on Earth. Her answer highlights the importance the connection between organisms and their food webs has to the planet:

> The ocean is the cornerstone of our life support system and the cornerstone of the ocean's life support system is life in the ocean. The ocean is alive. Oxygen is generated by living creatures. They are part of the system and food chains in the sea drive those systems. . . . Take away the ocean and we don't have a planet that works. Take away life in the ocean and we don't have a planet that works. All life needs water, but all life needs other forms of life to have the prosperous, complex communities of life, ecosystems of life that ultimately over four-and-a-half billion years arrived at a state that is just right for humankind.

Source: Anne A. McCormack. "Interview with Sylvia Earle." National Geographic Kids. National Geographic, 2013. Web. Accessed September 11, 2013.

What's the Big Idea?

Take a close look at Earle's answer. What is she trying to say about life on Earth? Pick out two details she uses to make her point. What does she mean when she says, "the ocean is alive"?

Invasive Plants

Scientists at the Smithsonian Environmental Research Center are studying a wide range of issues related to food chains and webs. Scientist John D. Parker is particularly interested in studying plants. Many plants are growing in new areas and entering food chains around the world. They cause problems when they take over a habitat and force out the native plants. Parker is trying to learn what makes these invading plants so successful.

Kudzu is an invasive plant in the southeastern United States.

Habitat Health

Scientists at Conservation International provide something called a Rapid Assessment Program. They study habitats and food webs around the world to check their health. A recent Rapid Assessment was completed at a new national park in East Timor, a small island country near Australia. Scientists spent two weeks studying, diving, videotaping, and photographing the fish and other ocean animals in the park. Their report will be used by East Timor to plan the laws and guidelines needed to preserve that sea life.

East Timor's coral reefs contain a huge variety of organisms.

Brown tree snakes are not considered dangerous to human adults, but their venom may harm children.

Controlling Snakes

The brown tree snake was accidentally brought to the island of Guam aboard cargo ships in the 1940s. This predator has eliminated almost all of Guam's native birds. Scientists are searching for ways to control the snake since it has no predators on the island. Their newest attempt is using mice treated with drugs as bait in snake traps. Mice are a favorite food of brown tree snakes, and the drug poisons them. Scientists hope this will help eliminate the snake population so the birds can return.

STOP AND THINK

Why Do I Care?

Parts of the world have living things and food chains that have not been studied. Sometimes they become extinct and their food chains break down before they are even discovered. Can you think of any reasons those disappearing organisms might be important to people? How might they affect your life? You may need to do a little more research to help you get started. Ask your teacher or a librarian for help.

You Are There

Imagine you are living during the 1600s when Europeans were settling the land in North America. Wolves and other large predators are living in the nearby forests. People are very angry because the wolves kill farm animals. They want to get rid of the wolves. After reading this book, what would you say to those people? Write down your thoughts and develop an argument that will convince them of your point of view.

Tell the Tale

Think of some animals that you see in your daily life. Then try to figure out where they fit into a food chain. Draw your food chain. In a paragraph or two, explain how energy moves through the food chain you drew.

Dig Deeper

After reading this book, what are some things you'd like to learn more about? Write down one or two questions that can guide you. Ask an adult to help you plan your research. You'll want to start online or in a library. Take notes about the new things you learn.

GLOSSARY

bacteria
tiny decomposers found in
most places on Earth

decomposition
breaking something down
into smaller parts

fungi
a group of decomposer
organisms that includes
mushrooms and their
relatives

larva
the stage of an insect's life
before it becomes an adult

nematodes
members of a group
of worms, including
roundworms and
threadworms

nutrients
substances organisms need
to live or grow

organisms
living things

photosynthesis
the process in which plants
use sunlight to create food
and oxygen

pollinator
an animal that spreads pollen
between plants, helping
them reproduce

scarce
few in number

tundra
a flat landscape with no trees
and frozen soil

LEARN MORE

Books

Capeci, Anne. *Food Chain Frenzy (The Magic School Bus Chapter Book)*. New York: Scholastic, 2004.

Crenson, Victoria. *Horseshoe Crabs and Shorebirds: The Story of a Food Web*. New York: Two Lions, 2009.

Web Links

To learn more about food chains, visit ABDO Publishing Company online at **www.abdopublishing.com**. Web sites about food chains are featured on our Book Links page. These links are routinely monitored and updated to provide the most current information available.

Visit **www.mycorelibrary.com** for free additional tools for teachers and students.

INDEX

ABOUT THE AUTHOR

Carol S. Surges has worked as a library media specialist for many years. In her spare time, if she's not in her gardens or on her bike, she enjoys writing and reviewing books. She lives with her husband in Wisconsin.